Chart
Your Way to
Success

GLENN
BLAND

Distributed By
INTERNET SERVICES CORPORATION
USA
BK393

POCKET GUIDES
Tyndale House Publishers, Inc.
Wheaton, Illinois

All Scripture in this book is from *The Living Bible*.

Chart Your Way to Success is adapted from *Success: The Glenn Bland Method*, © 1972 by Glenn Bland, published by Tyndale House Publishers, Inc.

Library of Congress Catalog Card Number 86-50652
ISBN 0-8423-0263-8
Printed in the United States of America

96 95 94 93
6 5 4

CONTENTS

Dream Success

If you were asked to define success, what would you say? Chances are you have never given it a great deal of thought.

There are probably as many different definitions for success as there are people in the world. Let us consider some of them.

A businessman might say that being successful means earning a lot of money.

A college football coach may believe the pinnacle of success is winning the National Championship.

To be successful, the pro athlete possibly desires to make the All-Pro team.

To a salesman, success means becoming the number one producer with his company.

Success to the housewife could be her role in her community's hospital auxiliary.

To the architect, success would probably be beautiful creations on his city's skyline.

A student's dream of success might be that golden moment when he receives his college degree.

The factory worker may feel successful

when he knows he has given his employer a good eight hours of work each day.

To an aspiring young lawyer, a desire to be president may be the ultimate success.

A dentist's dream of success could be a chain of clinics.

To the accountant, success could possibly mean his own office building.

To the minister, success might mean helping someone who is in need.

Success means many things to many people. Everyone may have a personal definition for success, but few have really thought the subject through. Success is more than any of the preceding definitions. It must be considered in greater depth and with a broader spectrum.

SUCCESS IS NOT . . .
Success is not merely "money grabbing." This is a shortsighted view because having money does not make a person successful. Al Capone was a millionaire and unsuccessful. One who retires at age forty by chiseling and cheating his or her way to the top is not a successful person. You cannot achieve true success by deluding others.

If you earned a million dollars, but lost your family and home and developed an ulcer in the process—you wouldn't be much of a success.

You would not be successful if you made a million dollars, but died of a heart attack at age forty-three simply because you burned the candle at both ends.

Neither is success living your life on "skid row" in the midst of poverty and disease, as some "anti-establishment" cults might suggest. Nature's laws are a greater force than the mere whims and wishes of man. Truth will always be truth and it cannot be changed.

SUCCESS AND BALANCED LIVING

True success avoids extremes! It is a journey. It is a gradual process. It abides in a realm in which balanced living is achieved. Through balanced living you will find happiness and success. Our Creator intends for you and me to lead happy and successful lives by applying the natural laws established by him.

This planet, called Earth, didn't just happen. It was created by an infinitely intelligent Being beyond our human understanding, and this Creator established certain natural laws that put order into all things. If you plan your life to function within the boundaries of these natural laws, you can achieve happiness and success. If you live outside these natural laws, you will never enjoy the inner peace, riches, enlightenment, and physical well-being for which you are searching. It is as amazing and simple as that.

If I were to choose one word to define our Creator, the word would be *balance*.

Our Creator

To take advantage of the natural laws of the universe, which will guide our lives to happiness and success, we must first understand the essence of the one who created them.

Sovereign: The Creator is the ruler of all things.

Righteous: It is impossible for the Creator to be wrong; he is perfect in every way.

Just: The Creator knows everything, all sides of every situation—therefore, it is impossible for him to be unfair.

Loving: The Creator gives perfect affection—a love beyond human love and understanding.

Eternal: The Creator has always existed, is very much alive today, and will always exist—he is everlasting.

Omniscient: The Creator knows everything—all ideas come from his infinite mind.

Think of the movement of the billions of heavenly bodies throughout the endlessness of space. Each is under perfect control just as precise as the movement of a fine Swiss watch. Consider the perfect balance between the plant and animal worlds, each complementing the other so that both will survive. Yes, our Creator has provided for everything.

SUCCESS AND BELIEF

Great people lead balanced lives made meaningful by belief. William B. Walton, president

Omnipotent: The Creator has the power to do anything—he is all-powerful and able.

Omnipresent: The Creator is everywhere at all times—he is not someone located in some remote, unknown place. He stands by your side.

Immutable: The Creator never changes—he is the same yesterday, today, and forever.

Truthful: The Creator is absolutely true—it is impossible for him to lie.

Now that you understand the essence of the Creator, you will find it much easier to understand why you can apply the natural laws of the universe in your life to accomplish your fondest dreams. The Creator is the source of every natural law leading to happiness and success. He has shared this wisdom with us and outlined his plan for the ages in an inspired book, *The Holy Bible.*

of Holiday Inns, speaking to the Tennessee State Convention of Optimists International, put it this way:

You have four great loves in your life:

1. Love of God. This love puts substance and meaning into your life. This great love enables a man to live with himself. This is the greatest among the four great loves. You must make a total commitment to this love.

2. Love of Family. The love of spouse, children, and relatives is encompassed by this love. This love must be a great love to avoid the problems faced by families in our modern society. It takes a total commitment to gain fulfillment from this great love.

3. *Love of Country.* You don't inherit a wonderful country like ours. It is passed on from generation to generation, but each new generation must earn the right to keep it. You must develop a fervent love for your country, if you are to be happy and enjoy the fruits of its plentiful bounty. Your love for your country must be a great love, a total commitment.

4. *Love of Work.* This must be one of your great loves for it provides the sustenance from which you live. To obtain this love you must engage in work that you enjoy and that is fulfilling. By making a total commitment to this great love you can guarantee yourself your share of prosperity.

During his speech, Mr. Walton constantly stressed the importance of attitude as being "the golden key that must be placed in the lock of life." The "Four Great Loves" are simply attitudes about life. His speech certainly exemplifies the thoughts of a man who knows the true definition of success.

Coach Vince Lombardi constantly guided his players with the following statement: "There are only three things that are important in your life: your God, your family, and the Green Bay Packers."

THREE KEYS TO SUCCESS
Success consists of three things:

1. *Direction.* Setting your sights on the things that are worthwhile in life and then establishing a plan to continuously work toward their fulfillment and accomplishment.

2. Balance. Keeping the proper perspective about every area of your life. Staying in harmony with nature's law, which produces perfect balance. Balance in all things brings about happiness.

3. Belief. Possessing faith. The greater a person's faith, the greater his degree of success. Successful people are believers!

With these three ingredients as a foundation, we will now establish our own definition of success. This will enable us to communicate with complete understanding as we continue through this book. When we refer to success, this is what we mean. Commit these few words to memory. You will carry them with you as a guiding light as long as you live.

Success is the progressive realization of predetermined, worthwhile goals, stabilized with balance and purified by belief.

Very few people really understand success. Now that *you* do—put it to work in your life!

KEY POINTS TO REMEMBER

- You cannot achieve true success by deluding others.
- Nature's laws are a greater force than the mere whims and wishes of man.

- Truth will always be truth and it cannot be changed.
- True success avoids extremes.
- Our Creator has provided for everything.
- Great people lead balanced lives that are made meaningful by belief.
- Success is the progressive realization of predetermined, worthwhile goals, stabilized with balance and purified by belief.

Think Success

Whatever your size, you possess in common with every other adult about forty-eight ounces of absolutely fantastic tissue. Carefully protected by the cranium, this is the most intricate and baffling computer ever conceived. This is your mind!

This fantastic computer of yours was designed and created by God's infinite intelligence. It is capable of processing data stored in the world's memory bank, which contains all information—from the past, the present, and on into eternity. Your mind can conceive of any idea you will ever need.

If one were to invent a mechanical computer with the endless potential of the human mind, the cost of using it would be so prohibitive that it would be impractical to put it into production. This may give you an idea of the value of the human mind, which despite its wealth-giving potential is used by most people at about 10 percent of its potential. We occupy our minds with insignificant things instead of letting them soar, as they were divinely designed to do, to accomplish big and important things.

Industry employs computer programmers to plan and screen information fed into computers. The computer can return information based only on the information it is given by the programmer. If the programmer does his work well, the information received will be worthwhile and useful; if he fails to write the program correctly, the information produced will be negative and useless.

The human mind is no different. Your mind is the computer and you are the computer programmer. If you put positive information in, the results will be positive and worthwhile. If you feed your mind-computer negative information, the results will be negative and directed toward failure.

Wisemen and philosophers throughout the ages have disagreed about many things, but they are unanimously in agreement on one point: *"We become what we think about!"*

Success Prompters

A man is what he thinks about all day long.
—RALPH WALDO EMERSON

A man's life is what his thoughts make of it.
—MARCUS AURELIUS

The greatest discovery of my generation is that human beings can alter their lives by altering their attitudes of mind.—WILLIAM JAMES

As a man thinks in his heart, so is he.
—PROVERBS 23:7

OUR PATTERNS OF THOUGHT

You *are* guided by your mind, and you must live upon the fruits of your thoughts in the future. Since "we become what we think about," it is most important that we carefully regard our thought patterns. This is one of the most powerful natural laws in the universe. You will find this law to be a two-edged sword—a natural law that can lead a man to a life of inner peace, wealth, enlightenment, and physical well-being, and a law that can lead him into the gutter into a life of misery.

How the law works for you depends on how you use it—for good or for evil; the choice is yours. Never forget that you live in a world of cause and effect—for every action, there is a reaction. Or as the Bible states it, "A man will always reap just the kind of crop he sows!" (Gal. 6:7).

Most of us try to change other people. To achieve our goals, we do not need to change others, we need to change ourselves. Others change as we change our thoughts about them.

Developing right thinking is not easy because it involves establishing new habits that take days, weeks, months, and often years before they become an integral part of our lives. New habits are not easily formed, especially when they must replace entrenched bad habits.

How do these bad habits and negative thoughts begin? Many times our minds are programmed with negative thoughts in childhood. An environment with negative people

Take the "Can't" Out of Your Life

History reveals that there have always been individuals who spend their lives in a negative world where *can't* is the most frequently used word in their vocabulary. Had such great men as Thomas Edison listened to the so-called experts of their day, our civilization would probably be regressing instead of progressing.

Here's proof. The following statements are taken from official documents, newspapers, and magazines widely read during their day. Listen to what the "authorities" had to say:

1840 *"Anyone traveling at the speed of thirty miles per hour would surely suffocate."*

1878 *"Electric lights are unworthy of serious attention."*

1901 *"No possible combination can be united into a practical machine by which men shall fly."*

1926 (from a scientist) *"This foolish idea of shooting at the moon is basically impossible."*

1930 (from another scientist) *"To harness the energy locked up in matter is impossible."*

There have always been those who said, "It can't be done." You can be sure of one thing—they did not understand one of the most important and basic natural laws of the universe: "Anything you can think of and believe in, you can achieve!"

influences us with its negativism. Certain books and magazines set us up for failure. Much of the entertainment available today has a negative impact on our thinking.

I could list numerous other reasons why a person lives in a negative world, but I am more interested in communicating to you the process of programming your mind with positive thoughts so you can build success in your life.

THE SUCCESS COMPLEX
Step 6 Mastery of the Details of Life
Step 5 Capacity to Love
Step 4 Relaxed Mental Attitude
Step 3 Inner Happiness
Step 2 Success-Oriented
Step 1 Success Doctrine (Wisdom)

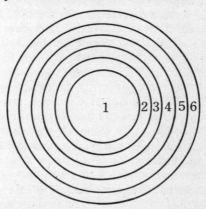

Step 1. Let us imagine for a moment that you are a master builder and you have been commissioned to construct a six-story building. You select the strongest supports and the best materials in designing the foun-

dation. Without a firm foundation, the structure cannot stand; it will crumble and fall. The full weight of the other five stories will rest upon this firm foundation.

Success doctrine is a strong foundation on which to build your future. The Bible says, "Wisdom gives a long, good life, riches, honor, pleasure, peace" (Prov. 3:16, 17). "He who loves wisdom loves his own best interest and will be a success" (Prov. 19:8).

You gain wisdom by becoming a student. You read, study, and listen each day on a planned and organized basis. The appendix has a list of books especially selected to provide you with a source of success doctrine. It must become a part of your life—you must eat, sleep, and drink success doctrine; it is good for the soul. "I, Wisdom, will make the hours of your day more profitable and the years of your life more fruitful" (Prov. 9:11).

Step 2. You will be success-oriented when you have success doctrine foremost in your mind. You will understand yourself, and because you do you can then begin to understand others. Your family life will improve, your business life will improve, your spiritual life will improve.

Step 3. Everyone in the world seems to be searching for inner happiness. You can find inner happiness as soon as you possess success doctrine and become success-oriented. Because you understand the Creator and his natural laws, your life will be in complete harmony with the world around you. This can generate an inner peace and happiness that will radiate forth like the glow of a candle in a window on a dark night.

Step 4. Once you have success doctrine in the frontal lobe of your mind and have become success-oriented and possess inner happiness, you will develop a relaxed mental attitude. You will be able to cope with every situation without frustration or anxiety. Virtually nothing will "shake you up" because you will possess a relaxed mental attitude. You will then have everything under control. The Bible says, "A relaxed attitude lengthens a man's life" (Prov. 14:30). Belief fosters a relaxed mind!

Step 5. The next important step in the success complex is acquiring the capacity to love. Do not confuse this with the selfish, humanistic love found so often in society today. If everyone had the capacity to love others, based upon the sure foundation of success doctrine, there would be no racial prejudice, no wars, no need for policemen, and everyone would respect everyone else for what he and she is. All the special gifts and powers from God will someday come to an end, but love goes on forever. "There are three things that remain—faith, hope, and love—and the greatest of these is love" (1 Cor. 13:13).

Even as great a man as the Apostle Paul readily admitted that without the capacity to love, everything else is meaningless. With success doctrine, you will have a much deeper and more meaningful feeling for your

19

family and the people around you.

Step 6. The pinnacle of the success complex is occupied by the mastery of the details of life, a gift to all who possess the success complex. Most people find it difficult to meet the daily trials and tribulations, but those who possess success doctrine know how to organize themselves through goals, plans, and priorities to handle anything that comes up.

The little things drive most people up the wall, but the individual with success doctrine accepts each little thing as a challenge. He learns to solve what he can and to live with what he can't without destroying his peace of mind.

THE PRICE OF SUCCESS

Most people want to be success-oriented, have inner happiness, display a relaxed mental attitude, possess the capacity to love, and be able to master the details of life. Few are willing to pay the price of gaining the success doctrine. They want to eat the frosting, but they don't want to take the time and trouble to bake the cake. The good things in life cannot be yours unless you pay the price to obtain them.

KEY POINTS TO REMEMBER

- We become what we think about!
- In the beginning you make your habits, but in the end your habits make you.

- Success doctrine will stabilize and sustain you through your greatest accomplishments and your bitterest adversities.
- The good things in life cannot be yours unless you pay the price to obtain them.

Get Set for Success

People with goals and plans succeed in life, while people without them fail. A leading New York medical doctor recently declared, "After examining 15,321 men and women in New York City, I came to see that the major problem of these patients was lack of values and objectives in life."

Thousands in the medical profession throughout the world could make the same statement. We are living at a point in world history when people restlessly wander about looking for something that can't be explained. They are confused, frustrated, filled with anxiety, and they can't understand why.

Goals and plans are the magic keys to happiness and success. Only 3 percent of all people have goals and plans and write them down. Ten percent more have goals and plans, but keep them in their heads. Eighty-seven percent drift through life without definite goals or plans. They do not know where they are going, and others dictate to them.

You must have goals and plans. Prisons are full of unfortunate people who had no goals and plans and one day each found himself outside the boundaries of man's laws. This would never occur to individuals with goals and plans established within the perimeter of those laws greater than man's— natural laws. Goals and plans made within the framework of natural law take the worry out of living. Conformity to God's laws frees your mind so that you may get on with your opportunities.

**Four Reasons People
Don't Set Goals**
1. They don't know how.
2. It's too much trouble.
3. They don't have faith in their goals and plans after they are developed.
4. They begin on a long-range basis and this prevents them from seeing immediate results, so they become discouraged.

If one of the above reasons is holding you back, the Bland Method of Goal-Setting and Planning will solve your problem. My method is the simplest and most efficient ever devised. It teaches you the principles of short-range and long-range planning, enabling you to discover immediately that planning really works.

WHEN PLANS SEEM TO FAIL
You will encounter temporary defeat many times, but by sticking with the program you

will charge through adverse situations like an All-Pro running back on his way to the goal line. Remember this principle: "Out of every adversity comes an equal or greater opportunity." It never fails.

This principle was clearly illustrated in Houston, Texas, several years ago. A great sports arena was planned, the first of its kind. A glass roof would cover the arena so that sporting events could be conducted under perfect climatic conditions despite Mother Nature.

When the magnificent structure was completed, Mother Nature retaliated. Grass would not grow on the playing field. The developers had a multimillion-dollar sports complex, built to house professional football and baseball, that had become worthless simply because grass would not grow.

Applying the principle, the builders attacked the problem. This adversity resulted in the discovery of an artificial playing surface that experts say is even better than grass. Today, artificial turf covers many out-of-door stadiums across our nation.

"Out of every adversity comes an equal or greater opportunity" is simply another way of saying that necessity is the mother of invention. You will find that what appears a permanent obstacle in the way of your desires is only a figment of your imagination. The Bible says, "You are a poor specimen if you can't stand the pressure of adversity" (Prov. 24:10). Welcome adversity; it is your springboard to great achievement.

Success Prompters
*It is better to aim your arrow at a star
and hit an eagle, than to aim your arrow
at an eagle and hit a stone.*—AUTHOR
UNKNOWN

*Assume in your imagination it is already
yours, the goal you aspire to have; enter
into the part enthusiastically, live the
character just as does the great actor
absorb the character he plays.*—RALPH
WALDO EMERSON

SHARE YOUR DREAMS

It is wise to seek the counsel of other qualified people when you set your goals and make your plans. In Proverbs 15:22 we find the following wisdom, "Plans go wrong with too few counselors; many counselors bring success."

I would suggest that you choose one or two individuals whose judgment and ability you greatly respect and form a Success Council for the purpose of exchanging ideas regarding each individual's personal goals and plans.

The Bible also says, "The intelligent man is always open to new ideas. In fact, he looks for them" (Prov. 18:15). So when you form your alliance, choose one or two others who can help you grow through the association. When two minds get together, their interaction seems to create a third "mind" that produces very creative thoughts and solves many problems.

How to Conduct a Success Council

1. To function properly, there must be complete harmony among its members.
2. There can be no negativism, or the group will become a negative force that will destroy each individual involved. To succeed, the Success Council must function in a proper positive atmosphere. Stay away from negative people because they will program you for failure.
3. Guide group thinking by establishing positive guidelines.
4. Schedule regular meetings with time for each member to make a personal progress report. This provides the follow-through necessary for individual goals and plans to become reality.

TIME YOUR DREAMS

Just setting a goal and making your plans to attain it are not enough. You must also decide when you wish to attain the goal. Set a date—it could be as short as an hour, a day, a week, or a month. It could be one year, five years, or at age sixty-five. Who knows? But you must establish this target date if your goal is to become a reality.

In 1960 President John F. Kennedy addressed the nation, announcing the beginning of a ten-year space program designed to put a man on the moon.

Let's analyze why this effort was such

a huge success. First, a definite goal was selected—a man on the moon!

Second, there was a basic plan to follow. Many problems were without answers, but there was a starting place—a basic plan.

Third, there was a target date—ten years in which to make this dream a reality.

There was a fourth procedure employed on this project. Although we have not yet discussed it, it is a fundamental part of goal setting. After the first three steps—a goal, a plan, and a target date—it was necessary to constantly keep the goal before them each day. This made it positive that the goal would become a reality. This principle is discussed at greater length in chapter 6.

Men and women engaged in the moonshot project worked together toward the fulfillment of their goal day by day. They did not know exactly how they would put a man on the moon, but they had faith and believed that it could be done. They did not know exactly what the spaceship would look like and they never conceived how great a part computers would play in the positive outcome of the project.

There were many unknowns, but they kept their goal constantly before them. They used group thinking and maintained their faith despite temporary defeat. Because they believed that their goal would be accomplished, the answers came and the United States successfully landed a man on the moon with one year to spare.

The tremendous achievement in reaching the moon should convince you that never again should you doubt the wisdom of goal setting and planning. The space program applied every principle for successful goal setting and so there was no way for the project to fail—a man was put on the moon!

Let me repeat the steps the space project took:

1. A goal was set.
2. A plan was made.
3. A firm target date was established.
4. Group thinking was employed.
5. Everyone kept the goal constantly in mind.
6. Action was applied.
7. They fervently kept the faith.

The result: It was impossible for them to fail!

KEY POINTS TO REMEMBER
- People with goals and plans succeed in life while people without them fail.
- Goals and plans are the magic keys to happiness and success.
- Goals and plans made within the framework of natural law take the worry out of living.
- Out of every adversity comes an equal or greater opportunity.
- You will find that what appears a permanent obstacle in the way of your desires is only a figment of your imagination.
- Dare to think big!

CHAPTER 4

Balance for Success:
Part One

Now we reach the most important phase of the goal-setting and planning process—the part that affects true happiness. The principles already presented will bring into your life an abundance of material wealth. But those principles will not bring happiness. True happiness can be achieved only by living a balanced life.

Have you ever watched a performer on a tightrope? He steps out firmly, but carefully. His balancing pole is tilted from side to side, ever so slightly, as he inches his way along. His eyes never leave the tightrope. They guide him to safety, just as surely as do his perfectly balanced muscles and movements. Diverting his eyes or exaggerating any movement can mean disaster, perhaps his life.

Balance is the key for the performer and for us. All of the natural laws brought into being by the Creator are based on the natural law of balance. Since the law of balance applies to all of nature—the universe, animal life, plant life, and everything that exists—it certainly applies to you and to me. When the law of balance is broken in the natural world—nature suffers! When the law of balance is broken in man's world—man suffers!

Each of us needs to learn to live within the boundaries of this great natural law. Guided by the law of balance in your life, you will create more happiness than you had ever dreamed possible. If you are in balance with the world around you, you will be happy! If you are out of balance with the world around you—you will be unhappy!

Let me show you how to use the law of balance in your life so that you may enjoy the abundant happiness that it will shower down upon you. Your life is made up of four major areas:

If you want true success and happiness, you must learn to set goals and make plans in each of these four areas. Without proper blend and emphasis upon these four areas, your life will be out of balance—you will be unhappy.

Let's explore each of these four areas that so vitally control your life.

SPIRITUAL GOALS

Do you know someone who is spiritually out of balance, someone so obsessed with things of a spiritual nature that he is a fanatic? As a result, people do not want to associate with him. They avoid him and he cannot accomplish his total purpose for one reason— he is overbalanced in one area.

Perhaps you know someone who, in great contrast, has no spiritual life. He leads a very loose existence and he is unhappy because he has no real friends. His activities are not conducive to founding genuine friendship. These examples are two extremes, but each illustrates clearly the problem of spiritual imbalance.

Any twentieth-century thinking man can arrive at an intelligent conclusion that there is a Supreme Being—a powerful God, an intelligent God with complete authority over all things.

The prophet Isaiah, in his inspired book in the Bible, records the following words from the Creator: "For there is no other God but me—a just God and a Savior—no, not one! Let all the world look to me for salvation! For I am God; there is no other" (Isa. 45:21, 22).

Man's very nature embodies an innate drive to worship something. This worship takes many different forms—both idealistic and materialistic—but the Bible says there should be only one object of worship and the true object is the Creator. When man's eyes are on the Creator, his life will flow with milk and honey!

FINANCIAL GOALS

Perhaps you have a friend who is financially out of balance. This individual is driven by money alone. Money is an obsession and the pursuit of it has caused a complete collapse of his personal life and family harmony. What's wrong? His life is out of balance!

Success Prompters

The rich man thinks of his wealth as an impregnable defense, a high wall of safety. What a dreamer!—PROVERBS 18:11

He who loves money shall never have enough. The foolishness of thinking that wealth brings happiness!—ECCLESIASTES 5:10

In the opposite extreme, you find an individual to whom money means nothing. He fails to provide for his own and he lives in poverty. He depends on charity to provide the necessities of life. Somewhere in between these two extremes there is a place of perfect balance—where you can have money and be happy!

The single biggest problem most people

face is the handling of money. They simply don't understand that they cannot have both money and things—at least, in the beginning! To accumulate money, you must give up things. But if you accumulate things, you will never have money. It is just that simple and yet few people really understand it.

King Solomon put it this way: "A man who loves pleasure becomes poor; wine and luxury are not the way of riches!" (Prov. 21:17). This came from a man who probably accumulated more riches than anyone in all history.

SEVEN STEPS TO ACQUIRING MONEY

1. Don't charge. Take your credit cards and hide them.

2. Don't consolidate your bills. Consolidating bills into one monthly payment at extremely high interest rates can create a new debt if your old, bad money management habits have not been changed.

If you are deeply in debt, work out a repayment plan and call all of your creditors and inform them of your plan and assure them that they will be paid. You will find them very willing to work with you.

3. Don't buy impulsively. When you desire to purchase anything of consequence, write it down on a chalkboard. Wait one month and then, if you still want it, consider working it into your budget. In most instances you will discover that your desire was only a passing fancy.

4. Establish a budget. Purchase a ledger

How Successful Were They?

In 1923, nine of the world's most successful financiers met at Chicago's Edgewater Beach Hotel. Financially, they literally "held the world by the tail"—anything that money could buy was within their grasp—they were rich—rich—rich! Read their names and the high position each held:

Charles Schwab, the president of the largest steel company.

Samuel Insull, the president of the largest electric utility company.

Howard Hopson, the president of the largest gas company.

Arthur Cutten, the greatest wheat speculator.

Richard Whitney, the president of the New York Stock Exchange.

Albert Fall, the Secretary of Interior in President Harding's Cabinet.

Jesse Livermore, the greatest "bear" on Wall Street.

Ivar Kreuger, the head of the world's greatest monopoly.

Leon Fraser, the president of the Bank

and begin to keep records of your income and expenses. Decide exactly what you will spend for necessities and luxuries each month and then stick with it. Watch every penny! A proven principle says, "If you can't live on $500 per month—you couldn't live on $5,000 per month." Your same old bad money management habits will cause you to overspend when earning $5,000, just as they of International Settlements.

A tremendously impressive group—right? Would you like to change positions with one of them? Before you decide, let's look at the picture twenty-five years later—in 1948:

Charles Schwab was forced into bankruptcy and lived the last five years before his death on borrowed money.

Samuel Insull not only died in a foreign land, a fugitive from justice, but was penniless.

Howard Hopson was insane.

Arthur Cutten became insolvent and died abroad.

Richard Whitney had just been released from Sing Sing prison.

Albert Fall had been pardoned from prison so he could die at home—broke.

Jesse Livermore committed suicide.

Ivar Kreuger took his own life.

Leon Fraser also committed suicide.

Now, are you still impressed with this group? A vast amount of talent and potential went down the drain with these men. What happened?

Their lives were out of balance!

did when you were earning $500. The only difference is that you will create much bigger problems when earning $5,000. It's true!

5. *Pay yourself first.* Every time you receive your paycheck, put something aside for yourself. At first, the amount may be small, perhaps only a dollar a week, but this will grow because you are forming a good habit—the habit of saving.

In Proverbs 21:20, we find this appropriate statement: "The wise man saves for the future, but the foolish man spends whatever he gets." Your creditors will wait for their money. They do not have any other choice. So pay yourself first—save!

Easy Ways to Save

Set an empty coffee can in your bedroom and empty into it the change from your pocket each night. When you cash a check, make it for a dollar more and put it into savings. Originate some games such as these and then play them to help you save money. Your goal should be at least 10 percent of your earnings.

---

6. *Pay monthly bills.* When you write checks each month, write them in this order:

   a. Church or some worthwhile charity.

   b. Savings.

   c. Insurance for security.

   d. Food.

   e. Shelter.

   f. All other things.

This procedure works like a charm. It will help you focus upon providing for the necessary things first and then letting all of the other things take care of themselves. Have faith; try it!

7. *Invest.* Permit me to outline for you five steps to good money management. This procedure has never failed to accumulate wealth. Putting these five steps to work will provide financial security in your life:

a. Basic needs. You must provide food, clothing, and shelter before investing in other things. Some never progress beyond providing these basic needs for their families. For those who do, the next step is:

b. Insurance. You must protect yourself from possible financial disasters with life, health, and casualty insurance. They protect you from financial ruin. Next comes:

c. Cash fund. As you grow financially, you need to build a cash fund for emergencies and opportunities that come along. Open a savings account and build it until it equals six months of your income.

Some people provide basic needs, insurance, and the cash fund, but never get beyond this level. For those who go beyond this step, the next one is:

d. Unimproved land. Investing money in unimproved land will provide a relatively safe investment with a very high return. The amount of land available is limited and as the population explosion increases, it will become more and more scarce.

Some people provide for the basic needs, insurance, cash fund, and unimproved land, and never proceed further. For those who do, the next step is:

e. Stocks and bonds. The final step in accumulating wealth is the purchase of stocks and bonds. This step can prove to be risky and caution should always be exercised when engaging in this type of investment.

These are the five steps to good money management. They will work for you to bring you the riches that they have brought many others. Don't be tempted to "make it quick" and jump all the way to step five. If you do, look out! You are headed for financial disaster. Stick with the five steps—they work!

SHARING THE WEALTH
No man can attain riches unless he enriches others. Study the success stories of the great men and you will find that many of them were very generous with their wealth. J. C. Penney and R. G. LeTourneau built vast wealth, but each attributed much of his success to sharing his good fortune with others.

I have discussed the principle of sharing with many successful businessmen. They have told me they would be literally afraid not to give—the consequences are too great. Happy and successful men will tell you quickly that "You can't outgive the Giver!" This is a natural law. This is referred to many times by the Bible and many other sources. "It is possible to give away and become richer! It is also possible to hold on too tightly and lose everything. Yes, the liberal man shall be rich! By watering others, he waters himself" (Prov. 11:24, 25).

I know men who give away 40 or 50 percent of their earnings and I have been told about others who give away four of every five dollars they earn. Naturally, these individuals are wealthy and can afford to give away much of their income, but these men have always made giving a habit—even when they were poor. Giving is one of the natural laws that they used to accumulate their wealth.

The Bible tells us that the Creator loves a cheerful giver and will return his gifts many times over if the gifts are given with the right attitude. You can't give with the expectation of getting. Your gift must be given freely with no strings attached. When gifts are given unselfishly, with nothing expected in return, they will be returned many times over. Gifts, without the proper attitude of giving, are meaningless.

The size of the gift is not important. But the attitude with which it is given is extremely important. If you give in the manner in which the Creator intends for us to give, you will be rewarded generously.

SERVICE: THE SOURCE OF MONEY

Money comes from some beneficial service you can render to your fellowman. You will be rewarded in direct proportion to the service you render—no more, no less!

Do you need to find some new service to render? Probably not. Most people can render a beneficial service in their present work. When men want to earn more money, their first impulse is to find a better job, a greener pasture. All too often, a change in occupation results in the discovery that the grass was not really that much greener on the other side of the fence. And, usually, the change has made things worse instead of better.

You probably have a virtual gold mine right where you are. Don't overlook the obvious. Establish your goals and make your plans to render the best possible service in your present work. If you should decide to change jobs later, you will be in a far better position to do so.

Get into the habit of doing more than you are paid for. One day you will be paid for more than you do. If you arrive at work early, stay late, and do a lot in between, you are sure to gain promotion.

If you don't receive one, then what? Wait a reasonable time, perhaps a year, and then talk to your immediate superior. Try to find out what the future may hold in the way of opportunities.

If you do not receive encouragement, then and only then would it be wise to explore the possibilities of finding other work.

Money will come to you on a sound basis and in large amounts in only one way. The formula? Service—success—then money.

Lasting success is a gradual process. It must begin with service; it can begin in no other way.

KEY POINTS TO REMEMBER
- When man's eyes are on the Creator, his life will flow with milk and honey.
- Most people simply don't understand that they cannot have both money and things.

- If you can't live on $500 per month—you can't live on $5,000 per month.
- No man can attain riches unless he enriches others.
- You can't outgive the Giver!
- Get in the habit of doing more than you are paid for. One day you will be paid for more than you do.
- Service—success—then money!

CHAPTER 5

Balance for Success: Part Two

It may seem to you that having discussed the importance of the first two areas for true happiness—*spiritual* and *financial*—that little else is required to be truly happy. To attain a true balance in life, two additional areas are essential.

The third area is *educational* and if this is not in harmony with the other principles your journey toward happiness will be erratic, if not impossible. The fourth area—*recreational*—meets the needs expressed in the old saying—"All work and no play makes Jack a dull boy."

EDUCATIONAL GOALS

Have you ever known an individual who was educationally out of balance? He has become so obsessed with gaining knowledge that he becomes an educated fool. He is so technical in his thinking that he forgets how to apply his knowledge in practical situations. He never seems to find a way to use knowledge to benefit him and his family. Education does not guarantee success; only the application of education will do that.

Then there is the individual who is illiterate; he possesses little or no education. Due to his lack of desire to educate himself, he and his family must suffer the consequences of insufficient education throughout their lives.

Both extremes illustrate educational imbalance. Somewhere between these two extremes, there is a place of perfect educational balance. You arrive at this point through goal setting and planning in the educational area.

TWO KINDS OF KNOWLEDGE
Generalized knowledge can help you become a more well-rounded person but it does not necessarily help you earn your living.

The knowledge that will guide you in your work and form the foundation for setting goals and establishing plans is called *specialized knowledge.* If you are a person of normal intelligence, having the willingness to work and the desire to obtain specialized knowledge, you can succeed!

Bill Roberts sells power tools. That's not all he does. Bill, according to his wife, eats and sleeps power tools, too. She may be exaggerating but Bill does spend his spare time keeping up with his business.

When a competitive line brought out a table saw several dollars under his price, he was concerned, but not for long. To achieve the price and to maintain a profit, the competitor had used bearings and other parts that made their saw not truly competitive with his saw.

Bill lost a sale to an old customer a few days after the new model came out. He did his best to persuade his customer to buy his brand but the price difference outweighed his statements about the inability of the new tool to stand up under constant use. When the tool burned out a bearing and overheated with use, the customer returned to the salesman who not only knew his own products but those of his competitors as well.

A salesman who knows only his own products has knowledge, but a salesman who knows his competitors' products as well has specialized knowledge in his field. Too many salesmen, unfortunately, lack even adequate knowledge of the products they sell. Without this knowledge, they must fail; without specialized knowledge, a salesman will not progress to the top. You can obtain this specialized knowledge through experience and study, just as Bill Roberts did.

Each of us should engage in at least one organized educational activity every year to keep our minds from becoming stagnant and unproductive. You can do this in several different ways—through formal classroom programs, correspondence courses, or individual study.

No matter which you choose, do it on a planned basis and for the purpose of gaining specialized knowledge. If you are a person of normal intelligence, having the willingness to work and the desire to obtain specialized knowledge, you can succeed!

RECREATIONAL GOALS

Have you ever known someone with a recreational imbalance in his life? There are two types. The first wants to play all of the time, never giving enough attention to the spiritual, financial, and educational areas of his life. This imbalance causes him to be an unhappy and frustrated person who never finds fulfillment in life.

I have a close friend of Waco, Texas, who at one time had a recreational imbalance in his life. He is one of the most talented and versatile men I have ever met. Charlie can do everything! He was an outstanding athlete in high school and college; he is a gifted musician; he is a par golfer; he is a champion bass fisherman; he can beat you at anything you want to do—anything from marbles to chess.

Having ability in such abundance created a problem for Charlie because his life's activity centered around his recreational pursuits, leaving the spiritual, financial, and educational areas to suffer. He was out of balance recreationally!

Charlie came to me several years ago. He said, "Glenn, I have been in the life insurance business for six years and I am worse off today than I was my first day in the field. I am either going to get in or out of the life insurance business! Can you help me?"

I replied, "Charlie, since you ask for help—I will help you." Although I had tried to help him before, he could never hear me.

Jesus said, "He that hath an ear, let him hear!" Each of us has ears, but very few of us can actually hear and understand the truth when it is presented. Usually a man must hit "rock bottom" before his mind is conditioned and receptive to hearing the solutions to his problems.

To make a long, long story short—Charlie heard! Man, did he hear! We went into a three-day goals-and-planning session behind the closed doors of my office. From that time forward, he has been a man with a mission in life. Today Charlie is a champion life insurance salesman.

Balance did it! Through the goals-and-planning sessions, all areas of Charlie's life were put into their proper perspective—putting balance into his life. As a follow-up to the initial thrust, we met weekly for a "truth session," as Charlie called it, to keep him on track.

In the second type of recreational imbalance, a person enjoys no recreational pleasures at all. He keeps his nose to the grindstone, never having enough time for such "foolish" things as physical exercise and relaxation. He also creates an atmosphere for serious problems in his life.

Every community has its Old Man Tom. As I describe him, you probably will think I am talking about someone you know. Old Man Tom is not old—in years—but he is in his ways.

The place he works just couldn't get along without Old Man Tom. He works early and late. He won't take a vacation. A holiday will find him spending half the day on the job. He takes the job home, too. Tom's wife listens to it on the daily rerun. In the morning he's grumbling about the problems he faces while he eats his breakfast.

No wonder they call him Old Man. He is old—set in his ways—mastered by his job. He is old physically, too, because he never does anything but work or sit and think about it. The last time he had any exercise was when he jumped to a conclusion. He doesn't know that adequate recreation would prolong his life, add happiness to his life, and, believe it or not, help him be far more valuable to the business.

These two extreme cases point up the need for the ideal situation, perfect balance. Planned recreation is very important to our physical and mental well-being. A strong body and a sound mind must function in complete harmony for success!

In the last two chapters you have been given many of the basic principles of the goal setting and planning process. A balanced life is so important that you should reread these chapters to keep these principles foremost in your mind. The Bible says, "Any enterprise is built by wise planning, becomes strong through common sense, and profits

wonderfully by keeping abreast of the facts"
(Prov. 24:3, 4).

Definite goals and plans are important to
you as an individual, but they are equally
important to your entire family. Setting family goals and establishing definite plans for
their fulfillment is a tremendous positive
force. You will find more detailed information
concerning planning in the next chapter.

No one can stop a man with a plan, because no one has a plan to stop him!

KEY POINTS TO REMEMBER
- Knowledge without application is useless.
- If you are a person of normal intelligence,
  having the willingness to work and the
  desire to obtain specialized knowlege, you
  can succeed!
- Choose a worthwhile goal and then re-
  lease yourself from your old self and go
  to that goal!
- A strong body and a sound mind must
  function in complete harmony for success.
- No one can stop a man with a plan, because no one has a plan to stop him.

Plan for Success

The Action Plan is the tool responsible for converting thought into action. Without a plan of action your goals would be meaningless and worthless. Start it now, even if you must begin on a very short-range basis. As you experience personal growth, it will be necessary to revise your plan of action periodically in order to keep it up-to-date and challenging. Remember to keep your plan before you each day. If you do, your goals will become a reality in your life.

COMPLETING YOUR PLAN OF ACTION

Set aside some uninterrupted time when you can devote all of your concentration and effort to working on the plan. Your action plan should include detailed goals and plans for both you and your family—they cannot be separated.

When completing the plan, commit yourself to the following:

1. Be perfectly honest with yourself.

2. Dare to think big.
3. Take action.
4. Believe in your plan.

YOUR PERSONAL AFFIRMATION

Write out a detailed description of the person you want to become, using chart 1 in the appendix. Consider the four areas of personal planning:

- What kind of person do I want to become spiritually?
- What kind of person do I want to become financially?
- What kind of person do I want to become educationally?
- What kind of person do I want to become recreationally?

Be very specific! Great care should be given to writing the description of the person you want to become because you will become that person! *Read this description each morning* to help you take up the role of this new person.

Consider these things when completing chart 1:

- How can I achieve peace of mind?
- What sort of work will I do?
- How much do I want to earn?
- What kind of home will I live in?
- How will I dress?
- What kind of automobile will I drive?

- What will others think of me?
- How will I help others?
- Will I be knowledgeable?
- What will I do for pleasure?
- Will I be balanced?
- Will I become wise?

WHAT IS YOUR PRESENT SITUATION?

Determine where you are presently so that you can establish sound plans to determine where you are going. Analyze each of the four areas of personal planning—spiritual, financial, educational, and recreational—in detail, using chart 2 in the appendix.

Is your present situation satisfactory or unsatisfactory? Then commit it to writing by checking one of the boxes and describing your present situation in detail be it positive or negative. Be honest with yourself as you write it down. Once you display the courage to admit the sort of person you really are, you will be well on your way to self-improvement.

Consider these things when analyzing your present situation in each of the four planning areas:

- Is my present situation satisfactory or unsatisfactory?
- What makes my present situation satisfactory?
- What makes my present situation unsatisfactory?

- How can I change my present situation?
- Do I lead a balanced life?
- Do I want to change my present situation?
- Am I straightforward and honest with myself?

SHORT-RANGE AND
LONG-RANGE GOAL SETTING

Each of the four areas of personal planning in charts 3-6 are separated into three divisions: One-Year Goals, Five-Year Goals, and Ultimate Goals. Through these three divisions you will be able to plan both short-range and long-range goals. Don't concern yourself if your goals are not elaborate in the beginning. That will come with time.

The three divisions of goal setting are as follows:

1. One-Year Goals. These are established on a calendar-year basis. Plan to accomplish them during the remainder of the current year.

These goals are very important because they are short-range and let you experience immediate results. Be very specific when setting one-year goals.

2. Five-Year Goals. These are classified as intermediate-range goals, based on current projections of your future potential. Adjust and update these goals every year so that they will remain in line with your personal growth. Decide where you want to be five years from now and then commit it to writing.

3. *Ultimate Goals.* These are long-range goals, lifetime goals. Project yourself on out to age sixty-five, seventy, or seventy-five, and give serious thought as to what kind of life you will want then. Also, think about all of the things you would like to accomplish during your lifetime.

YOUR SPIRITUAL GOALS

Keeping in mind your personal affirmation and the analysis of your present situation, begin to set goals in the spiritual realm of your life. The spiritual area of your plans is perhaps the most important, for it provides the belief and faith necessary for the achievement of all your goals in the other three areas of planning. Apply the procedure outlined in Short-range and Long-range Goal Setting regarding the three divisions of goal setting: One-Year Goals, Five-Year Goals, and Ultimate Goals. Consider these things when you are setting your Spiritual Goals:

- Do I give to worthwhile causes?
- Where can I go to receive spiritual growth?
- Where can I go to become involved in spiritually stimulating activity?
- Is my spiritual life balanced?
- Do I include my family in my spiritual plans?
- What do I want to do to make this a better world?
- Do I read and study the Bible?

- Do I meditate and pray?
- Do I believe in the Creator?
- How can I make a spiritual contribution of lasting value?
- How am I going to help others?

YOUR FINANCIAL GOALS

Keeping in mind your personal affirmation and the analysis of your present situation, you are now ready to establish your financial goals. Money is very necessary if you are to be happy and successful, but it must be kept in the proper perspective.

Apply the procedure outlined in Short-range and Long-range Goal Setting regarding the three divisions of goal setting: One-Year Goals, Five-Year Goals, and Ultimate Goals.

Consider these things when you are setting your Financial Goals:

- How much money do I want to earn?
- How much money am I going to save?
- How much money am I going to give to worthwhile causes?
- When do I want to retire?
- How much income do I want in retirement?
- What kind of work do I really want to do?
- Do I abuse the use of charge accounts and credit cards?
- Do I have a realistic budget for my family?
- Are all of my family's financial needs adequately met?

- What will be my net worth five years from now?
- What will be my net worth at retirement?
- Do I possess financial balance in my life?

YOUR EDUCATIONAL GOALS

Keeping in mind your personal affirmation and the analysis of your present situation, you are now ready to establish your goals in the educational area. Specialized knowledge will be very important as you progress toward the accomplishment of your goals. Mental growth is very necessary to great achievement. Please apply the procedure outlined in Short-range and Long-range Goal Setting regarding the three divisions of goal setting: One-Year Goals, Five-Year Goals, and Ultimate Goals.

Consider these things when you are setting your Educational Goals:

- Am I helping my family to set goals and make plans?
- Are my children going to college?
- Will I quit reading literary trash?
- Will I put only wholesome information into my mind?
- Do I have daily time for study?
- Am I going to achieve great wisdom?
- Do I know all there is to know about my work?
- Does my spouse have a program to gain mental growth?
- Will I share my knowledge with others?

- Can I force myself to become a student?
- Do I possess educational balance in my life?

YOUR RECREATIONAL GOALS

Keeping in mind your personal affirmation and the analysis of your present situation, you are now ready to set your recreational goals. A creative, success-oriented mind cannot function in a neglected body. Your body is the temple of your mind, so care for it well! Apply the procedure outlined in Short-range and Long-range Goal Setting regarding the three divisions of goal setting: One-Year Goals, Five-Year Goals, and Ultimate Goals.

Consider these things when you are setting your Recreational Goals:

- Do I have a personal fitness program?
- Do I enjoy personal recreation?
- Do I plan time for family recreation?
- What was my waist size when I graduated from high school?
- Do I take vacations?
- Do I do things that provide mental relaxation?
- Do I have regularly scheduled medical check-ups?
- Have I read *The Aerobics Way* by Kenneth H. Cooper, M.D.?
- Do I have fun in my personal and family recreation?

- Do I really want to be physically and mentally fit?
- Where can I become involved in worthwhile recreational programs?
- Am I living a recreationally balanced life?

YOUR MONTHLY
ACTIVITY CALENDAR

Now that you have made your personal affirmation, analyzed your personal situation, and set goals in the four areas of personal planning, it is time to take action. Begin by planning the most efficient use of your time on the Monthly Activity Calendar (pp. 70-81). These plans should be established on a calendar-year basis. You should begin today, and make plans for the remainder of the current year.

The following procedure should be used when completing your Monthly Activity Planner:

1. Photocopy the pages of the remaining months in the current calendar year for your use.

2. Write in the dates of each day of the remaining months in the small squares located in the upper left-hand corner of the larger squares.

3. You should now have a complete planning calendar for the remainder of the current year.

4. Now, go through each month day by day and plan all of your days off for the re-

mainder of the year. Be very honest.

If you are not going to work, please plan it just that way. Time off constitutes time that you will not be actively working at your job. Consider the following when planning your time off:

vacations
birthdays
anniversaries
recreation
rest
weekends
holidays
special occasions
conventions and meetings
parties

5. Now count the number of work days you have left to accomplish your objectives. Let *nothing* interfere with your planned work days. Let others plan their activities around you and your family.

6. Update your Monthly Activity Calendar. Enter any new activities on the calendar as soon as they are definite.

7. Count the number of off days on your Monthly Activity Calendar. Many times this is an eye opener to an imbalanced life.

8. Stick with your monthly plans once they are made.

9. Give copies of your monthly plans to *key people* to keep them informed.

10. Transfer your plans from your Monthly Activity Calendar to the Weekly Activity Planner.

11. Let your Monthly Activity Calendar guide all of your activity.

YOUR WEEKLY ACTIVITY PLANNER

Now you will become more specific with your planning process through the use of your Weekly Activity Planner. The procedure for making definite weekly plans is as follows:

1. Each week's planned activities should be taken from your Monthly Activity Calendar and transferred to your Weekly Activity Planner.

2. Place the week's date at the top of the planner.

3. Place your goals for the week at the top of the Planner.

4. List a minimum of *ten top-priority items* to be accomplished in any given week.

5. All activities in the four areas of your personal goals should be included on your Weekly Activity Planner.

6. Keep your Weekly Activity Planner visible at all times.

7. Any top-priority items that are not accomplished in a given week should be carried over to the following week for their fulfillment.

8. Your Weekly Activity Planner should be filled out during a time of quiet reflection at the end of each week. Always plan at least one week in advance.

9. Keep your Weekly Activity Planners so that they may be analyzed at the end of the calendar year to aid in helping you estab-

lish new plans. (*Note:* You may make your own Weekly Activity Planner or order one by writing Bland Institute, 7145 Chevy Chase, Memphis, Tennessee 38115.)

YOUR DAILY ACTIVITY PLANNER

The final step in the planning process is the Daily Activity Planner. This is the most important part of the planning process since this is your detailed action planner. It goes with you everywhere you go, guiding your destiny. You must use a Daily Activity Planner if you are to efficiently execute your Plan of Action. The procedure for using your Daily Activity Planner is as follows:

1. Each day's planned activities should be taken from your Weekly Activity Planner and transferred to your Daily Activity Planner.

2. You should set aside some time each morning to review your Weekly Activity Planner and fill out your Daily Activity Planner.

3. Place the day's date at the top of the planner.

4. Write out your goals for the day.

5. List the day's top-priority items.

6. Be very specific concerning information that is placed on the Daily Activity Planner—names, places, times, dates.

7. Include all activities on the Daily Activity Planner, even things as minor as "getting your hair groomed." Also all spiritual, financial, educational, and recreational plans.

8. Take the list of ten priority items from your Weekly Activity Planner and divide

them up by day for their accomplishment.

9. Include any special notes acquired during the day on the back of the Daily Activity Planner—names to remember, telephone numbers, business expenses, etc.

10. At the end of the day, take time to list your results on the back of the Daily Activity Planner. This will provide you a realistic look at your day's activity.

11. Write your favorite success prompter on the back of the Daily Activity Planner. Refer to it when strength is needed to carry on with the day's tasks. Everyone has favorite motivational sayings that mean a great deal to them, so write yours on your daily planner.

12. You should carry a copy of your Daily Activity Planner with you for quick reference at all times during the day.

13. Check off items from your Daily Activity Planner as they are accomplished.

14. Keep your Daily Activity Planners so that they may be analyzed at the end of the calendar year when new plans are being made. (*Note:* Planners can be ordered by writing the Bland Institute. Otherwise, you can make your own.)

YOUR FAITH CARD
You may want to carry a Faith Card (a motivational tool) with you each day to give you added strength in time of need. The Faith Card should be completed as follows:

1. List your major goals in your four planning areas.

2 Write the price you are willing to pay to accomplish these goals.

3. List the things you are thankful for.

4. List your latest great accomplishment.

5. List your favorite success prompter.

6. Complete your Faith Card expressing your own personal interest.

7. Read your Faith Card three times each day, morning, noon, and night. This procedure will "program" your subconscious mind.

8. Make a Faith Card for each month of the year and carry it with you at all times. It will give you courage when needed. (*Note:* Faith Cards may be ordered by writing the Bland Institute or you can make your own.)

Seven Steps to Success

1. *Let God guide you.* Get yourself out of the way and let the great, universal creative mind of God give you direction. Have faith.

2. *Establish a Faith Period.* Set aside thirty golden minutes each morning to engage in meditation and planning.

3. *Crystallize your goals.* Decide on specific goals that you want to achieve and keep them before you each day.

4. *Make a plan of action.* Develop a blueprint for achieving your goals and a target date for their accomplishment.

5. *Develop a burning desire.* Let your dreams for the things you want in life motivate you to action.

6. *Believe in yourself.* Use your God-given talents and abilities!

7. *Never give up.* Persevere in spite of the pressures of adversity. Success comes to persistent people!

Planning Charts

THE PERSON I WANT TO BECOME
CHART 1

_____
_____
_____
_____
_____
_____
_____
_____
_____
_____
_____
_____
_____
_____
_____
_____
_____
_____
_____
_____
_____

MY PRESENT SITUATION
CHART 2

Spiritual   Satisfactory   Unsatisfactory
_____
_____
_____
_____
_____

Financial   Satisfactory   Unsatisfactory
_____
_____
_____
_____
_____

Educational   Satisfactory   Unsatisfactory
_____
_____
_____
_____
_____

Recreational   Satisfactory   Unsatisfactory
_____
_____
_____
_____
_____

MY SPIRITUAL GOALS
CHART 3

One-Year Goals (Short-range Goals)

_____

_____

_____

_____

_____

_____

_____

Five-Year Goals (Intermediate Goals)

_____

_____

_____

_____

_____

_____

_____

Ultimate Goals (Long-range Goals)

By age _____ or in _____ years

_____

_____

_____

_____

_____

_____

MY FINANCIAL GOALS
CHART 4

One-Year Goals (Short-range Goals) _____
_____
_____
_____
_____
_____
_____
_____

Five-Year Goals (Intermediate Goals) _____
_____
_____
_____
_____
_____
_____

Ultimate Goals (Long-range Goals) _____
By age _____ or in _____ years
_____
_____
_____
_____
_____
_____

MY EDUCATIONAL GOALS
CHART 5

One-Year Goals (Short-range Goals)
_____
_____
_____
_____
_____
_____
_____

Five-Year Goals (Intermediate Goals)
_____
_____
_____
_____
_____
_____
_____

Ultimate Goals (Long-range Goals)
By age _____ or in _____ years
_____
_____
_____
_____
_____
_____

MY RECREATIONAL GOALS
CHART 6

One-Year Goals (Short-range Goals)

_____
_____
_____
_____
_____
_____

Five-Year Goals (Intermediate Goals)

_____
_____
_____
_____
_____
_____

Ultimate Goals (Long-range Goals)

By age _____ or in _____ years

_____
_____
_____
_____
_____
_____

MY MONTHLY ACTIVITY CALENDAR

JANUARY

Sunday	Monday	Tuesday	Wednesday	Thursday	Friday	Saturday

MY MONTHLY ACTIVITY CALENDAR

FEBRUARY

Sunday	Monday	Tuesday	Wednesday	Thursday	Friday	Saturday

MY MONTHLY ACTIVITY CALENDAR

MARCH

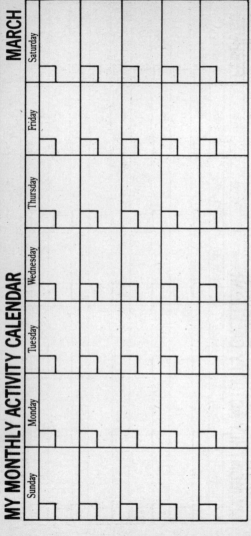

Sunday	Monday	Tuesday	Wednesday	Thursday	Friday	Saturday

MY MONTHLY ACTIVITY CALENDAR

APRIL

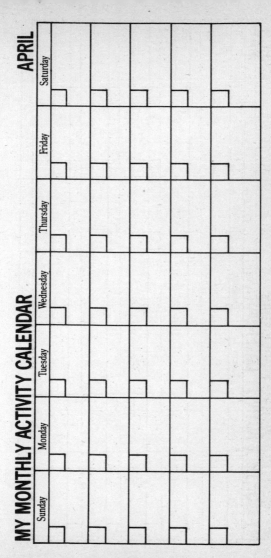

Sunday	Monday	Tuesday	Wednesday	Thursday	Friday	Saturday

MY MONTHLY ACTIVITY CALENDAR

MAY

Sunday	Monday	Tuesday	Wednesday	Thursday	Friday	Saturday

MY MONTHLY ACTIVITY CALENDAR

JUNE

Sunday	Monday	Tuesday	Wednesday	Thursday	Friday	Saturday

MY MONTHLY ACTIVITY CALENDAR

JULY

Sunday	Monday	Tuesday	Wednesday	Thursday	Friday	Saturday

MY MONTHLY ACTIVITY CALENDAR

AUGUST

Sunday	Monday	Tuesday	Wednesday	Thursday	Friday	Saturday

MY MONTHLY ACTIVITY CALENDAR

SEPTEMBER

Sunday	Monday	Tuesday	Wednesday	Thursday	Friday	Saturday

MY MONTHLY ACTIVITY CALENDAR

OCTOBER

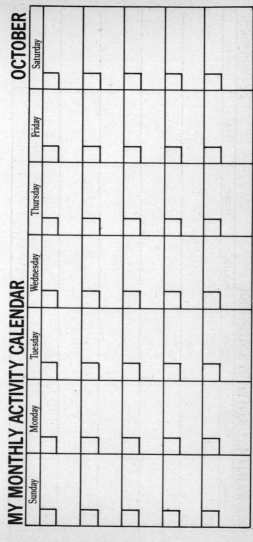

MY MONTHLY ACTIVITY CALENDAR

NOVEMBER

Sunday	Monday	Tuesday	Wednesday	Thursday	Friday	Saturday

MY MONTHLY ACTIVITY CALENDAR

DECEMBER

Sunday	Monday	Tuesday	Wednesday	Thursday	Friday	Saturday

Suggested Reading

Allen, Charles L. *God's Psychiatry.* Old Tappan, NJ: Fleming H. Revell, 1953.

Allen, James. *As a Man Thinketh.* Old Tappan, NJ: Fleming H. Revell, n.d.

Brande, Dorothea. *Wake Up and Live.* New York: Cornerstone, 1974.

Bristol, Claude M. *The Magic of Believing.* New York: Cornerstone, 1967.

Carnegie, Dale. *How to Win Friends and Influence People.* New York: Simon & Schuster, 1936.

Conwell, Russell H. *Acres of Diamonds.* New York: Harper & Row, 1915.

Dean, Dave. *Now Is Your Time to Win.* Wheaton, IL: Tyndale House, 1983.

Fromm, Erich. *The Art of Loving.* New York: Harper & Row, 1962.

Jones, Charlie. *Life Is Tremendous.* Wheaton, IL: Tyndale House, 1968.

The Living Bible. Wheaton, IL: Tyndale House, 1971. (I highly recommend the self-help edition. The happy and successful individual should read and study this book for the remainder of life!)

Mandino, Og. *The Greatest Salesman in the World.* New York: Bantam, 1974.

Otis, George. *God, Money and You.* Van Nuys, CA: Bible Voice, 1975.

Schuller, Robert H. *Self-love: The Dynamic Force of Success*. New York: Hawthorn, 1969.

Schwartz, David J. *The Magic of Thinking Big*. Englewood Cliffs, NJ: Prentice-Hall, 1959.

Steere, Daniel C. *I Am—I Can*. Old Tappan, NJ: Fleming H. Revell, 1973.

Taylor, Kenneth N., ed. *Who Is This Man Jesus?* Wheaton, IL: Tyndale House, 1967.

Wright, Norman. *Improving Your Self-Image*. Irvine, CA: Harvest House, 1977.

About the Author

GLENN D. BLAND is Chairman of the Board and Chief Executive Officer of United Financial Network, Inc., with national headquarters located in Memphis, Tennessee. He and his wife, Verna Beth, live in Memphis.

POCKET GUIDES
NEW FROM TYNDALE

■ *Action Plan for Great Dads* by Gordon Mac-Donald. A practical look at the essence of leadership in the home. Discover how to build character and confidence in your children. 72-0014-7 $2.25.

■ *The A-to-Z Guide for New Mothers* by Jayne Garrison. Take the worry out of motherhood! Here are suggestions on feeding the baby, assembling a layette, choosing a baby-sitter, and other helpful topics. 72-0008-2 $2.25.

■ *Chart Your Way to Success* by Glenn Bland. Make your dreams come alive with the help of this step-by-step plan tested by thousands of people. Features charts to help you set specific goals. 72-0263-8 $2.25.

■ *Demons, Witches, and the Occult* by Josh McDowell and Don Stewart. Why are people fascinated with the occult? This informative guide will answer your questions about occult practices and their dangers. 72-0541-6 $2.25.

■ *Getting Out of Debt* by Howard L. Dayton, Jr. At last, a no-nonsense approach to your money problems. Here's advice on creating a budget, cutting corners, making investments, and paying off loans. 72-1004-5 $2.25.

■ *Hi-Fidelity Marriage* by J. Allen Petersen. A respected family counselor shows you how to start an affair—with your own spouse. Learn how to keep love alive . . . rekindle old flames . . . grow from mistakes. 72-1396-6 $2.25.

■ *Increase Your Personality Power* by Tim La-Haye. Why do you get angry? Afraid? Worried? Discover your unique personality type, then use it to live more effectively—at home, on the job, and under pressure. 72-1604-3 $2.25.

■ *The Perfect Way to Lose Weight* by Charles T. Kuntzleman and Daniel V. Runyon. Anyone can lose fat—and keep it off permanently. This tested program, developed by a leading physical fitness expert, shows how. 72-4935-9 $2.25.

■ *Strange Cults in America* by Bob Larson. An easy-reading update of six well-known cults: the Unification Church, Scientology, The Way International, Rajneesh, Children of God, and Transcendental Meditation. 72-6675-X $2.25.

■ *Temper Your Child's Tantrums* by Dr. James Dobson. You don't need to feel frustrated as a parent. The celebrated author and "Focus on the Family" radio host wants to give you the keys to firm, but loving, discipline in your home. 72-6994-5 $2.25.

■ *When the Doctor Says, "It's Cancer"* by Mary Beth Moster. Cancer will strike approximately three out of four American families. Find out how to cope when you or someone you love hears this diagnosis. 72-7981-9 $2.25.

■ *When Your Friend Needs You* by Paul Welter. Do you know what to say when a friend comes to you for help? Here's how to express your care in an effective way. 72-7998-3 $2.25.